GAS BOOK 04

TOM HINGSTON STUDIO
CONTENTS

SHORT HISTORY
REPRESENTATIVE
COLOUR
PROJECT

Q&A

TOM HINGSTON STUDIO SHORT HISTORY

Tom Hingston hails from Lewisham, South London. At 16 he went to the London College of Printing to study BTEC in Graphic Design and Typography. The decision to leave school at this age and embark on a vocational path in education had been decided earlier on. Graphic design had been taught at a rudimentary level, as part of art classes, and this empowered Tom to explore it further - to become more aware of it. Investigations into education opportunities, at degree level, created a realisation of what a broad area this facet of the applied arts really was and how it impacted into other areas, photography for example, something which would ultimately colour his later work.

At the end of the 1980's, when Hingston was considering these opportunities, there was a very strong and clearly identified, visual awareness. Every part of culture was being looked at and re-fashioned in a more 'designed' image. Graphic design had now established itself as one of the leading disciplines in this regard.

The BTEC provided the practical grounding that would aid in his education in this discipline, forming the knowledge to take to degree level. The course at the London College of Printing was very structured, arming you with key skills to go out into the workplace, although not a place to explore your ideas or examine your thinking.

The college he selected for degree was Central Saint Martins. Pre-dominantly because the course at this college had an unrivalled reputation and secondly it was in London, a place that Tom felt, and still feels, contributes and feeds his interests and fascination with visual communication. On arriving at college the practical skills of the craft of graphic design were not shared by other students. The majority had come from foundation courses, which encouraged experimentation in all creative disciplines. They had not addressed the skills of the process. For Hingston this was of enormous benefit in knowing the rules and also having been regimentally taught in the ways of generating graphics mechanically, not digitally. This also meant that all these rules could now be broken, skewed or ignored in the more enlightened and liberated atmosphere he now found himself in. Jon Wozencroft lectured at Saint Martins and became Tom's personal tutor at a time when he was becoming increasingly disillusioned with his degree feeling that the course was not nurturing students' ideas, creating an atmosphere of complacency and neglect. Wozencrofts' intervention at this time encouraged Hingston in developing his ideas and re-igniting his enthusiasm.

The close relationship that he developed with Wozencroft developed further with an introduction to Neville Brody manifesting itself in employment at his studio upon graduating.

The period spent at the studio of Neville Brody covered a broad spectrum of projects, pre-dominantly for clients abroad. When Tom joined the studio had been renamed Research Studios and Brody was excited by the idea of a group of individuals coming together in a free-thinking environment with everyone's contribution having the same validity. The environment still felt like you were learning something. During that time, The Blue Note club opened, giving Tom the opportunity of doing free-lance work, along with other projects for friends, contacts he had made through enjoying club life in London. The balance between salary paid work and free-lance was tipping in the favour of projects completed after work. The hours spent working were getting longer and longer and decisions had to be made as to the next direction Hingston was to move in.

The confidence gained in his first full-time job made the break into his own studio immediate and comfortable. It was always really important to differentiate work from home. The normal route is to work from your home to keep your overheads to a minimum. There has to be a separation between the two spaces. Tom's approach has always been very labour intensive and this would not mix with fusing domesticity and work under one roof. His first workspace was to be found on Brewer Street in Soho, London, a location he has been in since. He was offered the space by Olly Buckwell of Dorado Records. The original space was a ground floor storeroom piled high with boxes of records. Buckwell suggested that he could tidy the boxes up, move them to one end, and put a desk at the other. A year and a half later Hingston had one other person working for him, Alyson Waller, along with having the boxes of records moved out and another desk moved in.

The first lesson to be learnt was that working for other studios meant a steady stream of work that would appear, as if by magic along with the comforting environment created by the presence of other human beings. Setting up as a company yourself magnifies the absence of these things along with being confronted by potential clients' reluctance to employ the services of one individual. Hingston found he was going to a lot of meetings and doing a lot of presentations and

REPRESENTATIVE COLOUR

not getting work. The client perception would be more people equalling a more robust organisation. For Hingston, a commitment to ideas and experimentation would be the building blocks for his company and not a desire to create a large organisation producing work purely to cover its costs.

Staff changes have been minimal since the company's inception. Alyson moved abroad with Danny Doyle being the next to join, contact being made after exhaustive searching and asking around. Shortly after Danny Simon Gofton also joined. Manuela Wyss was the last to join. She originally had been employed, on a free-lance basis, on a project for Penguin Books, and ended up staying. Selecting these people was a very hard choice. It has never been Hingston's intention to shift the emphasis onto him, as an individual, now that more people work in the studio, a space that has since moved upstairs into two rooms. He wanted a studio where the thinking is shared as a team of four people. Any bigger than it would be too hard to manage. To work for Tom Hingston requires an understanding of the craft of graphic design, a willingness to abstract it along with being able to introduce elements of your personal thinking.

PROJECT 01 DIOR

The worldwide advertising campaign for Christian Dior's womenswear represented a new departure for the studio. The opportunity of working with this fashion houses head, John Galliano, was an exciting prospect. Having previously worked with Nick Knight on Massive Attack a relationship had been forged that would benefit work with the House of Dior, a client of Nick Knight's. John had asked Nick if he could recommend potential art directors that they could work with. An interesting aspect to his selection was the fact that his portfolio did not contain any fashion work but represented a strain of problem solving that Dior were keen to take advantage of. This also came at a time in the studio's growth where there was a palpable desire to broaden the spectrum of clients and projects. This had also been frustrated by a number of potential clients not being able to make the mental leap between one discipline, i.e. music, and other areas, such as fashion. It is true to say

that Nick Knight played an important part in the decision making process for Dior and it was with a great sense of irony that his music work made him the ideal candidate when, in the past, it had frustrated his entry into this arena.

The creation of the work differed considerably from any other work. With music it's about a mood or feelings that you are extending. With fashion there are similar factors but you have a physical product to sell. This product has also got to be clear and evident in the images you create along with expressing the moods. The photography happens very quickly after the collection is shown on the catwalk. The thought process for both Nick and Tom is also very compressed with a heavy reliance on the spirit and energy John Galliano has brought to the House of Dior, a factor that is borne out of the clothing at all levels, from haute couture to ready to wear.

This energy, sprinkled with irreverence and excitement, is what is transferred into the imagery. The clothing has to appear in the advertising but Galliano is not scared of being playful in what he has created and is not precious with what are high value items. The idea is to conceive situations where this spirit can flourish and fun can be had. This work would also not take place if there were not a dedicated team of people that are bound up in this very labour intensive process. From hair to make up to styling and beyond the whole process has to function well in a pressured environment.

The relationship has extended into the perfume packaging for the fragrance Addict. It was felt that there needed to be more cohesion between the spirit of the campaign and the packaging. The final material selected reflected the pattern of light that was created in the photography and stripped the surface decoration to a minimum.

DIOR 'ADDICT' / Perfume Packaging   Christian Dior Parfums   2002   Design and Art direction: Tom Hingston Studio

1

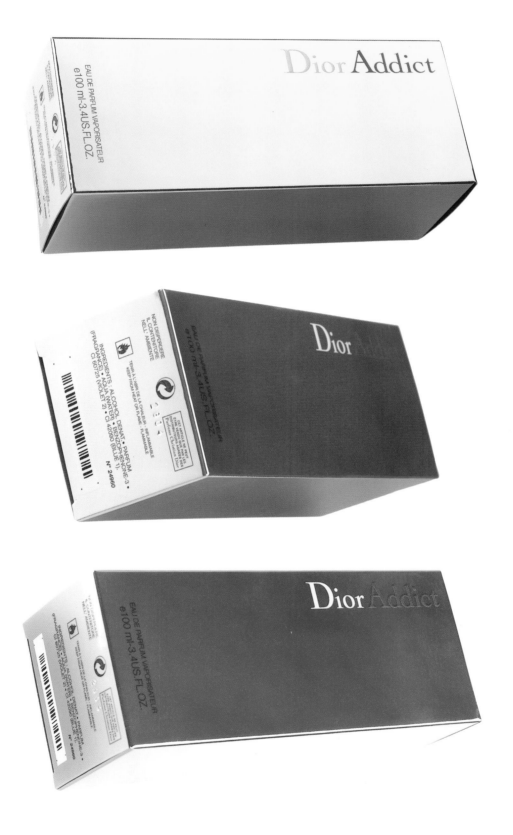

1			DIOR WOMENSWEAR ADVERTISING CAMPAIGN	Christian Dior	2001	Design and Art direction: Tom Hingston Studio
	1	2	SPRING / SUMMER 2002			Photography: Nick Knight
						Hair: Sam McKnight
						Make-up: Val Garland
2			DIOR WOMENSWEAR ADVERTISING CAMPAIGN	Christian Dior	2002	Design and Art direction: Tom Hingston Studio
			AUTUMN / WINTER 2002			Photography: Nick Knight
						Hair: Sam McKnight
						Make-up: Val Garland

PROJECT 02 ROBBIE WILLIAMS

This project, along with collaborating with Massive Attack, came in the same year. It all seemed to be going in a positive direction. After completing Mezzanine Tim Clarke and David Enthoven, who managed Robbie Williams, approached him with a project to design and art direct what was to become 'I've been expecting you'. It is interesting to draw some perspective over Hingston's career at this point. One could regard the projects he had undertaken, to this point, as somewhat esoteric and non-mainstream. Robbie Williams belongs firmly in the realm of pop music and nowhere else. For Tom this was a challenge.

Hingston was transfixed by Robbie's larger than life, dynamic personality. There was a sense that with him as a client you could change things and break a greater amount of rules when it came to his public persona. There was humour and vibrancy all centred around him.

The concepts presented were the most extreme situations one could find Robbie Williams in. There would be no beautiful portraits. Images of Williams being blown up or lounging around the pool of an expensive house ran counter to the received image of the airbrushed and manipulated persona of his former group Take That. You could argue that he has been given a character to play but for Hingston he is an entertainer who is role playing in situations. The choice of photographer Elaine Constantine was the perfect collaborator as her previous work

demonstrated all of the vibrancy that was needed.

For 'Sing When You're Winning' Tom collaborated with the fine artist Paul M Smith. Paul's work is principally about the exploration of the male ego and using himself as the subject in these photo portraits. He had completed a series of three works since graduating from The Royal College of Art, two series portraying soldiers and one of a men's night out on the town. The unusual aspect about his work is that he uses himself and no other people to create the different facets of the situation he is portraying and the personalities involved.

By this time his stature as a singer and celebrity had grown enormously and his image was very iconic, particularly in Europe. He was huge. He had become a character, partially created by himself and mainly built through the media. This was the inspiration for Tom where you would not even need to show his name, as he had become very much part of the fabric of consciousness. For Tom the multiple use of one face by Paul was the galvanising factor in facilitating this direction. There was a fear that because he was a formally educated artist with an impressive coterie of collectors then this commercial project would not interest him. However the reaction was immediately positive and was regarded as another series of working the ongoing exploration of an idea. The exploration of the ultimate male ego/icon. The final imagery was all based around

the different aspects of a football match. Not knowing a lot about the game both Tom and Paul had to spend a great deal of time researching matches and discovering a world neither of them knew a great deal about. The whole shoot took place over three days at Stamford Bridge.

The subsequent album Escapology, a title thought up by Robbie, came with an idea for discussion. The character of the world's greatest escapologist, Harry Houdini, was a person Robbie was interested in, coupled with the notion of being trapped. To create a series of scenarios, focusing on the notion of Robbie being ensnared in some way, gave the images a more modern slant and offered a more subtle reference to Houdini. It also gave it a more contemporary edge referencing modern escapologists such as David Blaine allowing a more contemporary spin on the images. Another interesting dynamic is that these people are never trapped or bound. It's showmanship. It's all a trick and could be said to refer to how Robbie presents himself in the media - inextricably linked and unable to remove himself, yet all the while in complete control of his destiny. Luis Sanchis took the photographs with Robbie being suspended 55 floors above Los Angeles. The rest of the images provide a surreal backdrop for him to appear trapped in. Through Sanchis' use of colour and composition the images are rendered beautiful and move away from the reportage of the previous album campaign. The image of Robbie still remains only this time you do not see his face.

| 1 | | 1 | ROBBIE WILLIAMS 'MILLENNIUM' / 60 × 80" Poster | Chrysalis | 1998 | Design and Art direction: Tom Hingston Studio Photography: Elaine Constantine |
| 2 | | 2 | ROBBIE WILLIAMS 'I'VE BEEN EXPECTING YOU' / 60 × 80" Poster | Chrysalis | 1998 | Design and Art direction: Tom Hingston Studio Photography: Elaine Constantine |

robbie williams

millennium

Coming 7.9.98 on CD/MC

robbie williams

I've been expecting you

www.robbiewilliams.com

sing when you're winning

1

	1	1	ROBBIE WILLIAMS 'SING WHEN YOU'RE WINNING' ALBUM / Campaign	Chrysalis	2000

Design and Art direction: Tom Hingston Studio
Photography: Paul M Smith

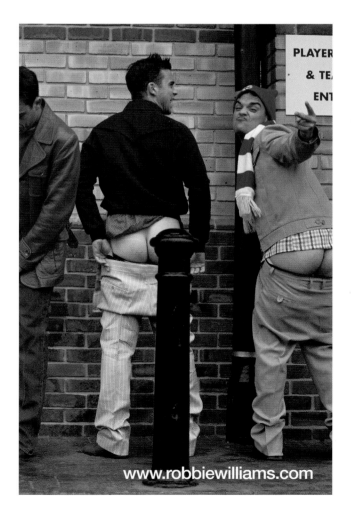

PROJECT 03 PORN?

Having seen Tom's music work Katy England and Emma Reeves of Vision On, the publishing arm of Dazed & Confused magazine, approached Tom with the idea of devoting a book to the subject of porn. At the outset they were undecided as to the direction this contentious theme would take the book content, but were excited to explore the possibilities Tom could bring to the project having been known in other areas of graphic design. From a brief requesting Tom to design the book he assumed sole responsibility as both Katy and Emma became occupied with other work, at a point when its future was questionable. Tom was now in charge of the commissioning and editing of the content along with art directing the project. The idea of asking a select group of image makers, whose work was known to Tom, made the approach to these individuals very personal, a method that was to colour the book, and also was the correct tactic given that the majority of the image makers selected have a personal attitude and language to their work and also could manage what is a very subjective and personal subject.

The selection comprised of people that Tom and Simon Gofton had worked with who he knew would respond to the subject in the way that he foresaw. It also gave him the opportunity of working with people whose work he admired or wished to work with. The brief was specific in that the work to be submitted had to be original along with a need to emphasise the question mark in the title. The question mark reflects that personal nature of any individual's attitude or response, a response that can never be predicted allowing a platform for the rich subject matter to be explored.

Some ideas and responses were very rapid allowing for a period of refinement and also creating a dialogue. Others had an immediacy that meant that their acceptance did not need any discussion. Because of the disparate nature of the responses, along with where they were in the world meant that the project took two years to complete. The order takes the reader through a series of senses and feelings along with the pace jumping from fleshy to sensual to the explicit. This would then be contrasted with images that were deemed to be more personal or humorous. For Tom the notion that the book is erotic is not a subject he will be drawn on but the breadth of imagery heightens what pornography is. It is your own judgement that is brought to bear with regards to the subject and is not something that is forced on you. It is also important to point out that the ratio between male and female contributors was evenly split.

The choice of a Pink, leather/flesh like cover material is self-explanatory given the subject matter. The typography on the cover alludes to the notion of forbidden fruit. The text section was French folded with quotations hidden on the reverse of each page adding to another theme of pornography, that of things being hidden or waiting to be discovered. The choice of the art historian and critic Mark Irving gave an added intellectual weight to the book without being overwhelming in its use of theoretical writing. It was also important for the text not to have the writers' personality stamped on it but to simply reference the content by comment or comparison. The book was not without its production problems with a number of printers, around the world, refusing to print the book because of its content, with even the artwork being stopped in customs when a printer was found. The book's delivery to the United Kingdom was also marred.

The evolution of the studio allowed this project to appear organically within the development of his work. It is representative of a growth within the area of collaboration where Tom has actively pursued the establishment of a broad base of contacts who he can work with. This makes the approach to this project not that of a book designer but as an extension of the development of the studios activities and its public perception.

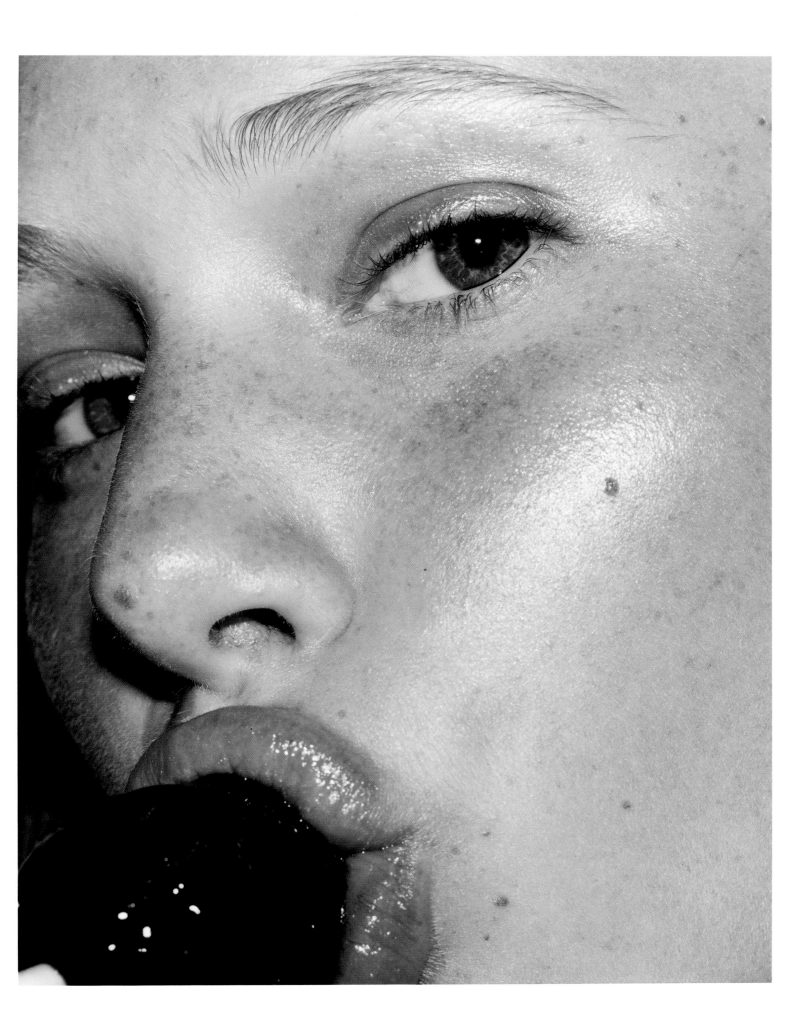

1

2

1	2

IMAGE TAKEN FROM 'PORN?'

IMAGE TAKEN FROM 'PORN?'

Photography: Anuschka Blommers and Niels Schumm

Photography: David Hughs

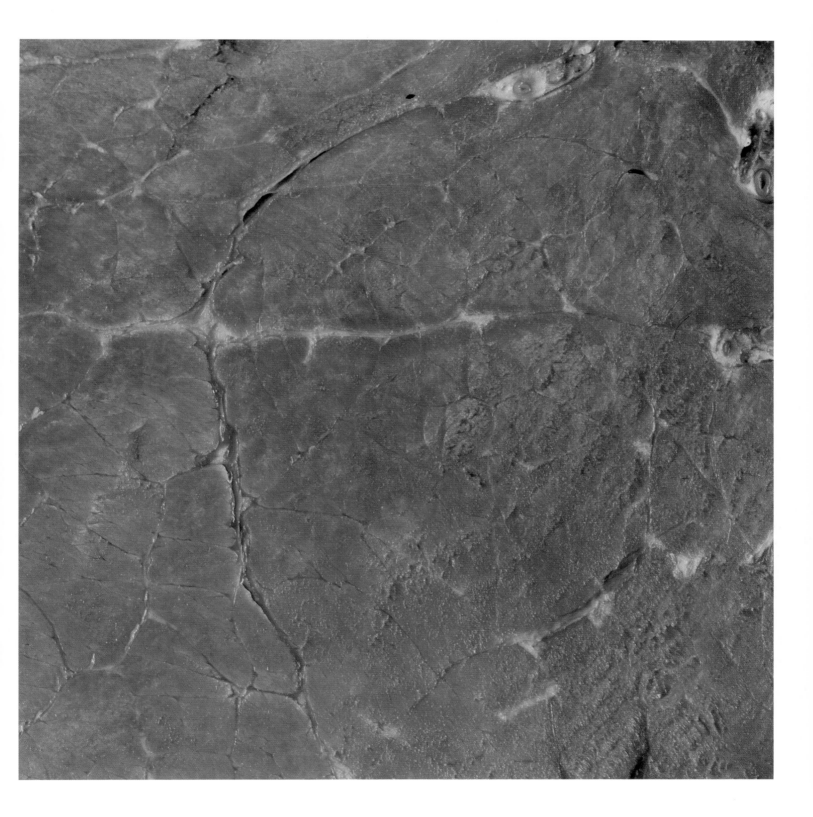

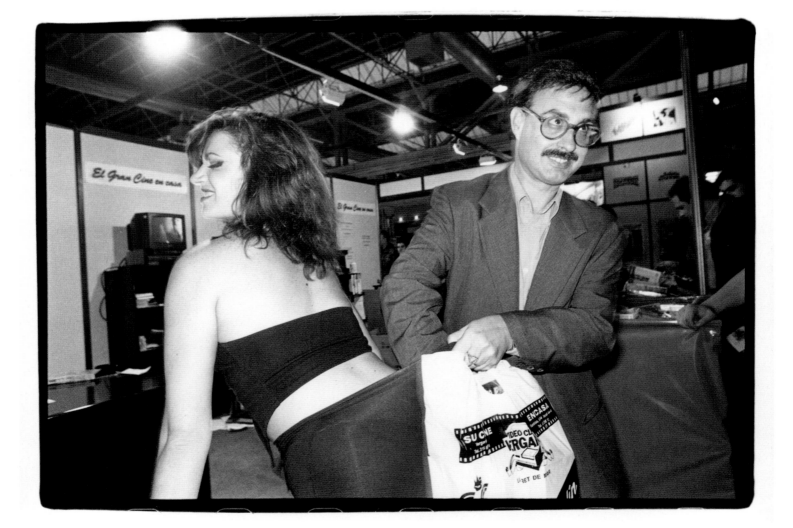

| 1 | | | IMAGE TAKEN FROM 'PORN?' | Photography: Derek Ridgers |
| 2 | 1 | 2 | IMAGE TAKEN FROM 'PORN?' | Photography: Greg Fay |

IMAGE TAKEN FROM 'PORN?'

IMAGE TAKEN FROM 'PORN?'

Photography: Gemma Booth

Photography: Larry Sultan

1

2

1	2

IMAGE TAKEN FROM 'PORN?'

IMAGE TAKEN FROM 'PORN?'

Photography: Luis Sanchis

Simon Foxton and Stephen Male

PROJECT 04
MASSIVE ATTACK

Through a mutual friend Hingston was introduced the band's manager, Marc Picken. Massive Attack were completing work on their fourth album and beginning to think about its sleeve design. The group, Robert Del Naja in particular, have always been very involved in the process and artwork. The band were looking to establish a relationship with an individual or small studio that they could have an on-going dialogue with - which extended beyond just the album and into other areas from stage visuals to websites.

The style of Mezzanine would not have been realised without an acute awareness of the themes and ideas around the music. There was no brief as such; it was about Tom working closely with Robert until they found they had established specific themes and ideas that represented the album. Hingston had met Nick Knight through a mutual friend, just prior to being commissioned. At this meeting they had spoken about the possibility of working together. Massive Attack provided the opportunity. In the early stages of image gathering Nick volunteered his services as part of the research

process.

Mezzanine is neither one place nor another. It also suggests hybrids in some way, a split-level between two places. The insect was used to create something recognisable and twisting it in some way, causing damage to it. The perception is multi-layered and one of tension. The images of insects were very beautiful yet very dark. The inclusion of smashed car-parts in place of limbs and joints answered the original idea along with a sense of vulnerability caused through this damage. All the insects were sourced by Knight from the archive of The Natural History Museum in London. The images of car parts were photographed in a breakers yard. The smashed up cars had been attacked with axes and hammers rendering them almost unrecognisable. With covers such as Teardrop there is also an ambiguity as to what is actually represented which adds to the beauty of all of these Black and White images.

This project was then followed by the Singles compilation after a small period of time. The brief was to create something that was very

special. It was important that the opportunity of creating special packaging was not just for the sake of it and wouldn't appear contrived. The use of the heat sensitive ink plays on the fact an individual has to handle the box and it responds to the heat of the hand. That also allowed Hingston to further explore the subject of layers, an aspect that had begun with Mezzanine. The sleeves for each CD feature Robert Del Naja's artwork, giving it a sense of history.

The Massive Attack DVD is yet another body of work that needed to be held in one package. It was a departure from the Singles Collection along with being a humorous comment on the state of DVD packaging, a new area of music packaging that had already become incredibly homogenised - the book in the card box with posters and extras on the disc. The idea was to do the complete opposite and strip everything away leaving a disc of raw data. If it were possible to exclude the bar code and certification logo then they would have. One could also argue that it is part of a desire to strip everything one perceives about this group and their music - to start with a blank page.

| 1 | | MASSIVE ATTACK 'MEZZANINE' / Album Cover | Virgin | 1998 | Design and Art direction: Tom Hingston and Robert Del Naja
Photography: Nick Knight |
| 2 | | MASSIVE ATTACK 'MEZZANINE' / 60×80" Teaser Poster | Virgin | 1998 | Design and Art direction: Tom Hingston and Robert Del Naja
Photography: Nick Knight |

ANGEL
MASSIVE ATTACK 13.7.98
THE NEW SINGLE ON CD.12″. MC FEATURES REMIXES FROM BLUR & MAD PROFESSOR

TEAR DROP

MASSIVE ATTACK 27.4.98

CD.12". MC FEATURES REMIXES FROM PRIMAL SCREAM & MAD PROFESSOR

SINGLES 90-98
MASSIVE ATTACK 7.12.98
AVAILABLE ON CD - BOXED SET FEATURES 11 CD's / 63 TRACKS
VINYL - LIMITED EDITION / NUMBERED VINYL BOXED SET

HEAT SENSITIVE PACKAGING

Massive Attack end of tour party in association with
Respec Radio & Bristol Royal Hospital for Sick Children
LAKOTA 6 Upper York Street, Saturday 19 December
10 pm → 4 am info: 0117 9426208 DJ's: Mushroom,
The Underdog, Rob Morris, Daddy G, Nick Warren,
Task & Bear, Queen B, Peter D

Exchange your ticket stub from any Massive Attack Show at the Anson Rooms
for entry to the party: £5.00 charity donation mandatory:
*Entry STRICTLY LIMITED to first 700 applicants.

MASSIVE ATTACK / MELANKOLIC PRESENT:
DJ's: LIAM HOWLETT, JAMES LAVELLE, LEWIS PARKER
16.12.99

10 PM Until Late @ The Dojo Lounge Bristol.   Admits 1 only.

PROJECT 05 BLUE NOTE

The Blue Note club was formerly a jazz club called The Bass Clef on the corner of Hoxton Square. It was later bought by the record label Acid Jazz who renamed it. At that time it was the only club in the area, to be visited after you had been to The Bricklayers Arms, a pub around the corner. The heavy commitment of running a record label meant that someone was needed to manage its affairs, on a full-time and committed basis. A sense of integrity and vision was required to give it some significance. Sav Remzi was then employed to push this project forward. He had gained a reputation for running a club called the Red Eye in South London, putting on nights for DJ's such as Andy Weatherall and Giles Peterson. He had also recently started a record label called Nuphonic with Dave Hill. A friend of Toms, Ross Allen, introduced him to Sav. He had been looking for someone to address the identity of The Blue Note as the previous design had been put there in somewhat of a hurry.

The initial relationship was just to create the identity but Tom was increasingly drawn into the plans for the clubs, the nights and events that were being planned, in particular. The name Blue

Note is synonymous with a particular genre of jazz music, which created its own visual style in the 50's and 60's with a series of elegantly designed sleeves. For Hingston the intuitive response was to create something that he regarded as the polar opposite of what this name signified. Remzi's approach to the club programming was very fluid - a melting pot, and Tom was keen to capture this in the logo, principally through the ever-changing shape or form that surrounded the logo. This fluidity further expressed itself in the visual language of the flyers.

The brief for each flyer was normally based around the printing specification in terms and number of colours. There would be no other detail leaving it to intuition and the period of time, sometimes two hours or an evening, to complete it. By the end of the week Hingstons work would be scattered over Hoxton Square. For Tom this method of working on project was stimulating and cathartic, the work having such a short life span. Having been working on projects which took months, at Research Studios, the thinking process for flyers ran counter to these projects which came into being in the evening hours.

Collaboration with illustrator Ian Wright on some of the flyers also allowed Tom to draw on Ian's musical knowledge in creating the designs. The Far East nights, run by Giles Peterson, gave opportunities to be playful with the ideas on the notion travel. Anokha was a genre of music also demanding a certain visual style fusing Asian and Western influences. Regardless of which night they were for they are visual statements with a very short life span. Due to the frequency there was never any time to have the designs discussed or approved, along with Tom factoring some period for him to assess the design he was creating. The flyers were a place where all the fragments of ideas, which could not be used on large projects, could be utilised. The colour palette was a personal choice setting it aside from other flyers of the time. Because there were so many it allowed him to experiment and not feel limited in picking the types of colours one normally associates with flyers. One could argue that experimentation was still taking place when the flyer had been printed. This was borne out by some of the reactions Hingston got from what had been produced, severe in some cases. But it is such a temporary medium mistakes and risk taking is affordable.

foreignEXPOSURE

foreignEXPOSURE ◉
The Blue Note 1 Hoxton Square London N1 6NU T: 0171 729 8440

Processed

The Embassy presents PROCESSED @The Clinic 13 Gerrard Street, London W1 10pm > 3.30am £7/£5 conc. + Drinking card holders

Saturday 5 July
Talvin Singh (Anokha)
Dave Hill (Nuphonic)
Tom Hingston (London Xpress)

Saturday 2 August
Jools (Nightmares on Wax)
Andrea Parker (MoWax)
Tara Strong (Cup of Tea)

Saturday 6 September
Richard Fearless (Death in Vegas)
James Prentice (Acid Jazz)
Burro (Happiness Stars)

Forthcoming DJ's for October, November & December: Jon Carter (Monkey Mafia), Andy Weatherall (T.B.C) Athletico, Mekon (Wall of Sound) Visuals: Tom Hingston
+ Resident Embassy DJ's: Gino Silano, Michael & Louise, Dave Krysko, Tara Strong, Jason, John Cooke

nuphonic

ustar+nuphonic Sat 30th November 10pm-5am Entry £8/£6 conc

To celebrate what has been an excellent year for music, two of London's independent labels give you their first ever joint party. The music will reflect the styles that have influenced the labels and help to shape their sounds. It will take in Boogie and Dub Disco through to todays Funky House Fusion. From the U Star team are Dan & Conrad commonly known as the Idjut Boys. Whilst flying the flag for Nuphonic are Simon Blaze Action Lee, plus David Hill & Jools Butterfield from the label. Upstairs Crispin J. Glover & DJ D will be delivering an alternative selection that will be less dance floor orientated but every bit as Funky. At The Blue Note 1 Hoxton Square London N1 6NU T: 0171 729 8440. Nearest Tube: Old Street. (Parking Limited)

↑ **LIFT** ON TWO FLOORS WITH RESIDENT DJ'S: DR BOB JONES, EARL, CATFISH & DAMON HALVIN, WITH GUESTS:
SATURDAY 5TH APRIL: OLEN GUNNER | SATURDAY 3RD MAY: ALAN RUSSELL | SATURDAY 7TH JUNE: LOFTY
10PM-5AM £10/£5 CONCS. AT THE BLUE NOTE, 1 HOXTON SQUARE, LONDON N1 6NU. PARKING LIMITED

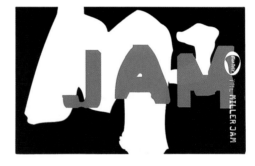

THE GALAKTIC Soundlab

The Blue Note presents...THE GALAKTIK Soundlab. Saturday 13 September 10pm 5am - £10/£8 concs/members

Each month the Blue Note and the Galaktics reach out to invite musically like-minded artists from all over Europe to expose their sound, and inject an alternative influence to London....with resident DJ's collective and je gooster (mixing on a decks) plus MC NYA &MGM trio providing a bass heavy heavy mix of Jazz and Breakbeats live on stage. Joined by special guest Ben Wilcox October 11th - special guest to be announced

The Blue Note 1 Hoxton Square London N1 6NU T: 0171 729 8440

Blue Note | SONY

what makes you think you're so special?

sony & the blue note: together fusing technology, fine art and fashion design.
launch night: wednesday 10 july 1996 9.00 pm - 3.00 am
entrance only with this invite. DJ's on the night: DJ Linford, Dave Tipper and DJ Tamsin.
featuring customisers: alexander mcqueen, bording, holmes, mtv, gimme 5, savage,
patrick cox, hussein chalayan, rifat ozbek, diesel, w&lt, grifin, antonio berardi,
acupuncture, stephen bliss and vexed generation + the special collective:
cosmo sarson, nathan jenden, joanna fox, mike pigneguy and nathan kelly.
drinks will be provided.

July 11 -August 2 1996. @ 1 hoxton square. london n1 6nu. T: 0171 729 8440 gallery open weekdays 12pm – 6pm

JAM THE MILLER JAM

AFRIKA BAMBAATAA AND TIME ZONE

THE BLUE NOTE & COLD SWEAT PRODUCTIONS PRESENT:
THE GODFATHER OF HIP-HOP & RENEGADE OF FUNK HITS THE BLUE NOTE FOR HIS ONLY DATE IN LONDON.
COME & TASTE THE BEST GOOD TIME, OLD SKOOL ATMOSPHERE THAT ONLY BAMBAATAA & HIS TWO DECADES ON THE MIC CAN PROVIDE, TOGETHER WITH TIME ZONE IN THE GROOVE BESIDE HIM. THE BIG MAN IS BACK. PLUS DJ PATRICK COLDSWEAT. AT THE BLUE NOTE. No. 1 HOXTON SQUARE, LONDON N1 6NU. TELEPHONE 0171 729 8440 XTRA £3.00 ON THE DOOR PAYS ENTRY TO MAGIC BUS 'TILL FIVE AM. TICKETMASTER 0171 344 4444

afrika bambaataa LIVE WEDNESDAY 5 MARCH 1997 @THE BLUE NOTE 1 HOXTON SQUARE LONDON N1 6NU TELEPHONE: 0171 729 8440

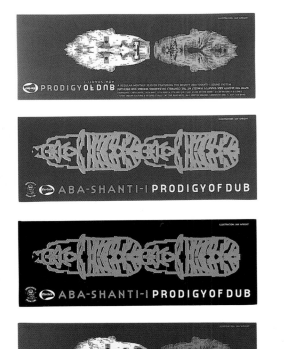

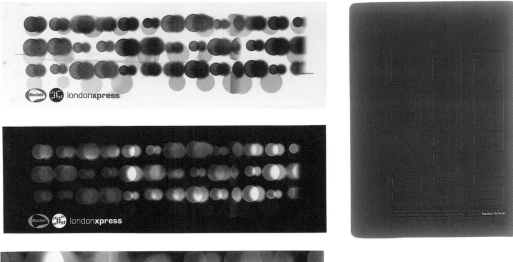

1			'PRODIGY OF DUB' / Flyers	1996	Design and Art direction: Tom Hingston Studio Illustration: Ian Wright
2	1	2	'BLUE NOTE CLUB' / Monthly Programmes	1997	Design and Art direction: Tom Hingston Studio
3	3		'LONDON XPRESS' / Flyers	1996	Design and Art direction: Tom Hingston Studio

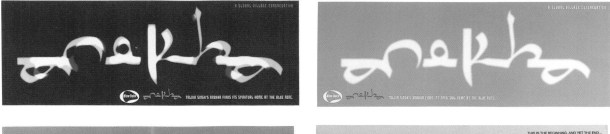

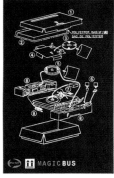

1			'ANOKHA' / Flyers	1996 / 1997	Design and Art direction: Tom Hingston Studio
2			'MAGIC BUS' / Flyers	1996	Design and Art direction: Tom Hingston Studio
3			'HI-HAT' / Flyers	1996	Design and Art direction: Tom Hingston Studio
4			'FREE RADICALS' / Flyers	1996	Design and Art direction: Tom Hingston Studio

PROJECT 06 NUPHONIC

Founded by Dave Hill by Sav Remzi in the mid 1990's, Nuphonic was a small dance music label created as a project without large ambitions. With Sav looking after the Blue Note and Dave DJ'ing it was not a top priority with three or four releases a year by friends and associates. Its success was optimised through the national and international reputation the Blue Note was beginning to garner.

The history of music has a heritage of beautiful sleeve art, something contemporary dance music had not yet fostered. For Dave Hill sleeve art was very important. He wanted the label to have a visual integrity on par with the music and he was instrumental in shaping this need for the next 5 or 6 years.

As with the Blue Note flyers Tom was given complete freedom along with less restrictive budgets and deadlines. The artists also respected Nuphonic's choice of visual identities for their releases. For Dave Hill the briefing process would be accompanied by presenting a number of visual references he saw as part of the music. This would create a grounding for other ideas to grow from. The first sleeves had the appearance of being very structured, similar in style to the Blue Note flyers, building graphic compositions and layers.

With the first compilation the style altered to a sole use of type. The music was varied with all of the artists having different sleeve art, hence the

peeling way of any visual material, as such. The solution is neutral and does not suggest musical style or genre, creating a democratic and beautiful object, beauty and tactility - marking the early sleeves.

The early sleeves did not rely on any collaboration with other image-makers, Tom preferring to retain control over each project partly for financial reasons, partly because the work was so linked to his Blue Note projects. With the success of the label, more releases and a broadening of the music that was being output it became more applicable to collaborate with people to capture the mood and themes of the artists.

1			'LAST NIGHT A DJ SAVED MY LIFE' / CD Cover	2000	Design and Art direction: Tom Hingston Studio
2		2	'NUPHONIC 04' COMPILATION / 12" Sleeve	2001	Design and Art direction: Tom Hingston Studio
	1				

Nuphonic 04   Including tracks from
Maurice Fulton,
Block 16 and
Justin Robertson

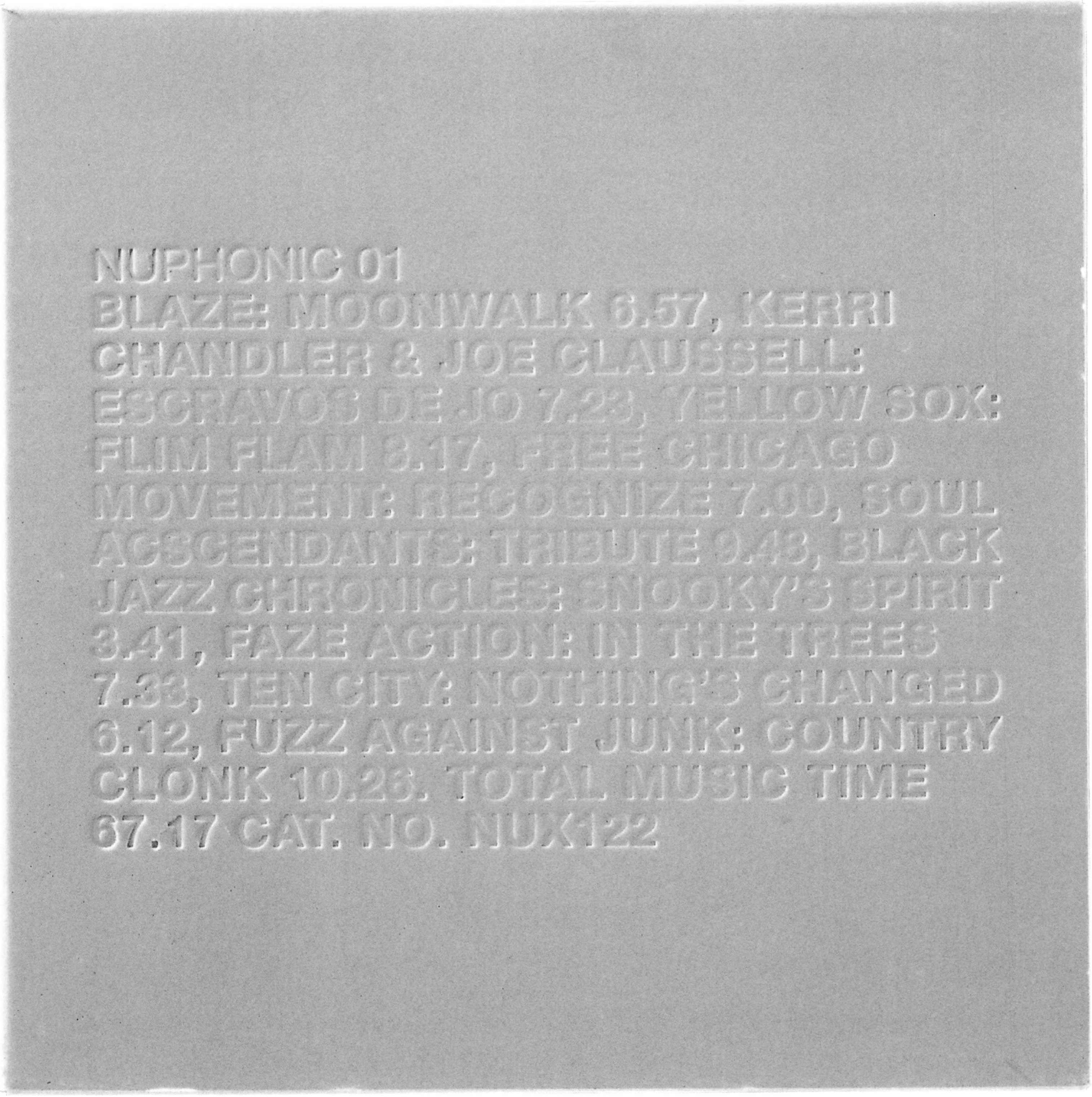

NUPHONIC 01
BLAZE: MOONWALK 6.57, KERRI
CHANDLER & JOE CLAUSSELL:
ESCRAVOS DE JO 7.23, YELLOW SOX:
FLIM FLAM 8.17, FREE CHICAGO
MOVEMENT: RECOGNIZE 7.00, SOUL
ACSCENDANTS: TRIBUTE 9.48, BLACK
JAZZ CHRONICLES: SNOOKY'S SPIRIT
3.41, FAZE ACTION: IN THE TREES
7.33, TEN CITY: NOTHING'S CHANGED
6.12, FUZZ AGAINST JUNK: COUNTRY
CLONK 10.26. TOTAL MUSIC TIME
67.17 CAT. NO. NUX122

| 1 | | | 'NUPHONIC 01' COMPILATION / CD Cover | 1998 | Design and Art direction: Tom Hingston Studio |
| 2 | 1 | 2 | 'NUPHONIC 02' COMPILATION / 12" Sleeve | 1999 | Design and Art direction: Tom Hingston Studio
Photography: Richard Green |

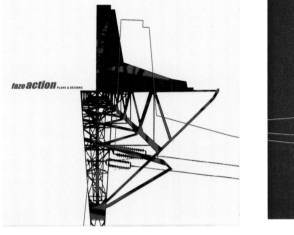

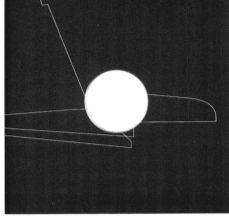

1			FAZE ACTION 'PLANS AND DESIGNS' / CD Cover	1997	Design and Art direction: Tom Hingston Studio
2			FAZE ACTION 'GOT TO FIND A WAY' / CD Cover	1999	Design and Art direction: Tom Hingston Studio Photography: Richard Green
3			FAZE ACTION 'KARIBA' / CD Cover	1999	Design and Art direction: Tom Hingston Studio Photography: Richard Green
4			FAZE ACTION 'MOVING CITIES' / CD Cover	1999	Design and Art direction: Tom Hingston Studio Photography: Richard Green
5			FAZE ACTION 'MOVING CITIES' / CD Cover	1999	Design and Art direction: Tom Hingston Studio Photography: Richard Green
6			FAZE ACTION 'SAMBA' / CD Cover	1999	Design and Art direction: Tom Hingston Studio Photography: Richard Green

Key grid:
```
      1
  2   3   4
  5   6
```

Justin
Robertson
Presents
Revtone

22–10–01

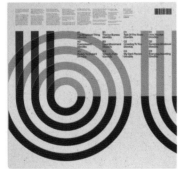

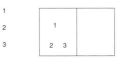

1			'JUSTIN ROBERTSON PRESENTS REVTONE' / A2 Poster	2001	Design and Art direction: Tom Hingston Studio
2	1		'JUSTIN ROBERTSON PRESENTS REVTONE' / 12" Sleeve	2001	Design and Art direction: Tom Hingston Studio
3	2	3	'JUSTIN ROBERTSON PRESENTS REVTONE - THE BRIGHTEST THINGS' / 12" Sleeve	2001	Design and Art direction: Tom Hingston Studio

BLOCK 16 CAN'T STOP
WITH ROBERT OWENS

BLOCK 16 FIND AN OASIS
FEATURING JHELISA

BLOCK 16 MORNING SUN

The debut album from Block 16
featuring collaborations with
Jhelisa, Bim Sherman,
Jon Lucien and Robert Owens

Out Now

www.nuphonic.co.uk

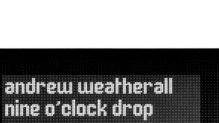

andrew weatherall
nine o'clock drop

andrew weatherall
nine o'clock drop

Double vinyl/CD   Featuring:
Released 17.07.00   23 Skidoo
                     Torch Song
                     (William Orbit)
                     A Certain Ratio

1		BLOCK 16 'CAN'T STOP' / 12" Sleeve	2001	Design and Art direction: Tom Hingston Studio Illustration: Danny Boons
2		BLOCK 16 'FIND AN OASIS' / 12" Sleeve	2001	Design and Art direction: Tom Hingston Studio Illustration: Danny Boons
3		BLOCK 16 'MORNING SUN' / 12" Sleeve	2001	Design and Art direction: Tom Hingston Studio Illustration: Danny Boons
4		ANDREW WEATHERALL 'NINE O' CLOCK DROP' / 12" Sleeve	2000	Design and Art direction: Tom Hingston Studio Photography: Dan Holdsworth

PROJECT 07
OTHERS

A. It's Automatic   B. Holiday Home
Zoot Woman are Jonny Blake, Adam Blake and Stuart Price.
All tracks written and produced by Zoot Woman.
Published by Warner Chappell/Copyright Control.
℗ and © 2000 Wall Of Sound Recordings. Made in England.

For further information and licensing contact:
Wall Of Sound, Office 3, 9 Thorpe Close, London W10 5QZ.
Email: general@wallofsound.uk.com
Website: www.wallofsound.net

Design: Tom Hingston Studio.

1			ZOOT WOMAN PROMO / 7" Sleeve	Wall of Sound	2000	Design and Art direction: Tom Hingston Studio
2	1	2	ZOOT WOMAN 'LIVING IN A MAGAZINE' / 12" Sleeve	Wall of Sound	2000	Design and Art direction: Tom Hingston Studio
						Photography: Sølve Sundsbø

Living In A Magazine

1			HORACE ANDY 'LIVING IN THE FLOOD' / CD Cover	Melankolic	2000	Design and Art direction: Tom Hingston Studio
	1					Photography: Pete Moss
2	2		FILTER 'ELVIS NEVER MEANT SHIT TO ME' / CD Cover	Filter	1998	Design and Art direction: Tom Hingston Studio

1			X-PRESS 2 'I WANT YOU BACK' / 12" Sleeve	Skint	2002	Design and Art direction: Tom Hingston Studio Photography: Jason Evans
2		1 2 3	X-PRESS 2 'LAZY' / 12" Sleeve	Skint	2002	Design and Art direction: Tom Hingston Studio Photography: Jason Evans
3			X-PRESS 2 'MUZIKIZUM" / 12" Sleeve	Skint	2002	Design and Art direction: Tom Hingston Studio Photography: Jason Evans

spacek
how do i move/
getaway

The new single on CD and 12"
Released 20–05–01
Featuring remixes by Attica Blues and Jay Dee

| 1 | | | SPACEK 'HOW DO I MOVE' / 30 × 20" Poster | Universal / Island | 2001 | Design and Art direction: Tom Hingston Studio |
| 2 | | | SPACEK 'CURVATIA' / CD Cover | Universal / Island | 2001 | Design and Art direction: Tom Hingston Studio |

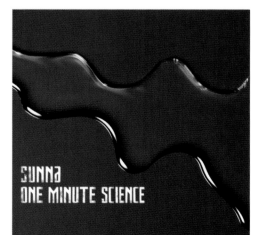

1		SUNNA 'ONE MINUTE SCIENCE' / 30×20" Poster	Melankolic	2000	Design: Tom Hingston Studio Photography: Guido Mocafico
2		SUNNA 'ONE MINUTE SCIENCE' / CD Cover	Melankolic	2000	Design: Tom Hingston Studio Photography: Guido Mocafico
3		SUNNA 'POWER STRUGGLE' / CD Cover	Melankolic	2000	Design: Tom Hingston Studio Photography: Guido Mocafico
4		SUNNA 'I'M NOT TRADING' / CD Cover	Melankolic	2000	Design: Tom Hingston Studio Photography: Guido Mocafico

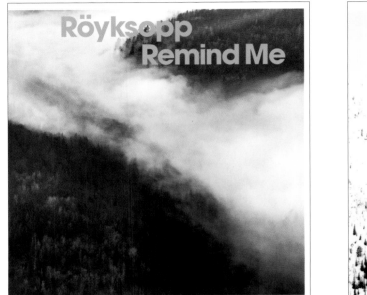

1				RÖYKSOPP 'REMIND ME' / 12" Sleeve	Wall of Sound	2001	Design: Tom Hingston Studio Photography: Sølve Sundsbø
	1	2					
2	3	4		RÖYKSOPP 'EPLE' / 12" Sleeve	Wall of Sound	2001	Design: Tom Hingston Studio Photography: Sølve Sundsbø
3				RÖYKSOPP 'MELODY A.M' / 12" Sleeve	Wall of Sound	2001	Design: Tom Hingston Studio Photography: Sølve Sundsbø
4				RÖYKSOPP 'POOR LENO' / 12" Sleeve	Wall of Sound	2001	Design: Tom Hingston Studio Photography: Sølve Sundsbø

1	CUSTOM BLUE 'ALL FOLLOW EVERYONE' / 12" Sleeve	Universal / Island	2002	Design and Art direction: Tom Hingston Studio Photography: Jason Evans
2	CUSTOM BLUE 'EP ONE' / 12" Sleeve	Universal / Island	2002	Design and Art direction: Tom Hingston Studio Photography: Jason Evans
3	CUSTOM BLUE 'EP TWO' / 12" Sleeve	Universal / Island	2002	Design and Art direction: Tom Hingston Studio Photography: Jason Evans
4	CUSTOM BLUE 'SO LOW' / 12" Sleeve	Universal / Island	2002	Design and Art direction: Tom Hingston Studio Photography: Jason Evans

```
 1  2
 3  4
```

1 TETRA SPLENDOUR 'MR BISHI EP' / 7" Sleeve   EMI   2000   Design and Art direction: Tom Hingston Studio

1

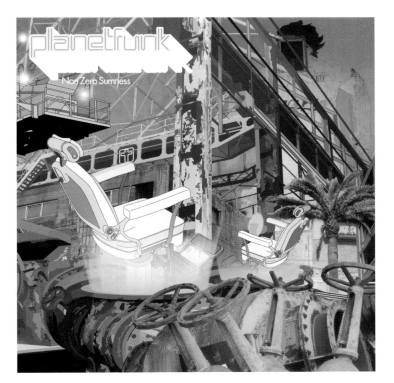

1			PLANET FUNK 'INSIDE ALL THE PEOPLE' / 12" Sleeve	Virgin	2001	Design and Art direction: Tom Hingston Studio Illustration: Kam Tang
2			PLANET FUNK 'NON ZERO SUMNESS' / 12" Sleeve	Virgin	2001	Design and Art direction: Tom Hingston Studio Illustration: Kam Tang
3			PLANET FUNK 'THE SWITCH' / 12" Sleeve	Virgin	2001	Design and Art direction: Tom Hingston Studio Illustration: Kam Tang

| 1 | | | HARVEY NICHOLS BIRMINGHAM BROCHURE | Harvey Nichols | 2001 | Design and Art direction: Tom Hingston Studio |
| 2 | 1 | 2 | HARVEY NICHOLS EDINBURGH BROCHURE | Harvey Nichols | 2002 | Design and Art direction: Tom Hingston Studio
Photography: Mario Godlewski |

HARVEY
NICHOLS
EDINBURGH
2002

03

Harvey Nichols
Autumn/Winter 2001
Introduction

Okay, let's admit it, Harvey Nichols is the best
shop in the world to buy clothes. Whether you're
in London or in Leeds, it's all there. Contemporary,
Casualwear, Formalwear and Accessories. What
more do you want?

Cover: striped t-shirt £80, striped tank top £90,
pinstriped jacket £475, bleached jeans £115,
all by Martin Margiela. *Above:* checked
shirt £90, cord jacket £295, cord trousers £130,
all by Dufier of St George.

Harvey Nichols
Autumn/Winter 2001
Accessories/Underwear

You want more? Find all the modern luxurious items
you could ever want: ties by Gucci, Bill Amberg
wallets, cufflinks by Tateossian, and a whole range
of goodies from Dolce & Gabbana. Not to mention
shoes and undies.

Vest £18.95, shorts £18.95, all by Dolce & Gabbana

HARVEY NICHOLS MENSWEAR CATALOGUE   Harvey Nichols   2001   Design and Art direction: Tom Hingston Studio
Photography: John Spinks

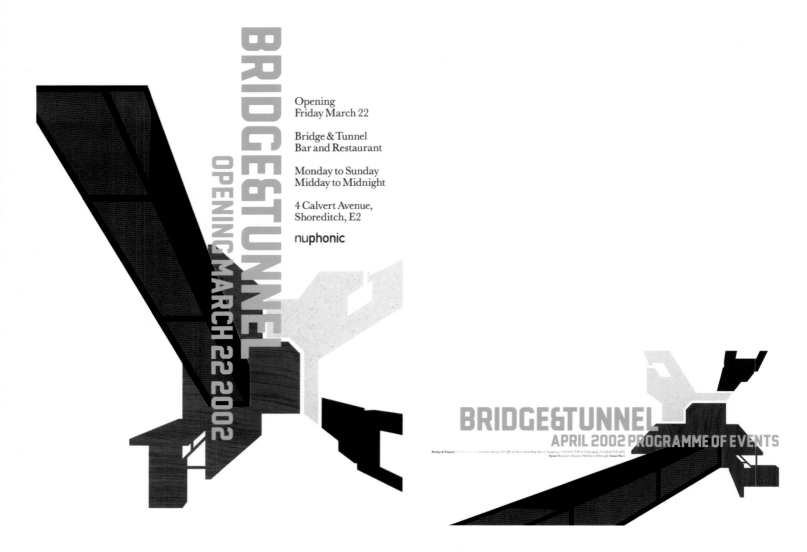

Opening
Friday March 22

Bridge & Tunnel
Bar and Restaurant

Monday to Sunday
Midday to Midnight

4 Calvert Avenue,
Shoreditch, E2

nuphonic

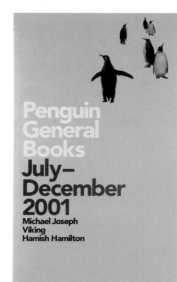

1			BRIDGE & TUNNEL / A2 launch poster and flyer	Bridge & Tunnel	2002	Design and Art direction: Tom Hingston Studio
2	1		'JULY-DECEMBER 2001' / Penguin Books Catalogue	Penguin	2001	Design and Art direction: Tom Hingston Studio
3	2 3		'JANUARY-JUNE 2001' / Penguin Books Catalogue	Penguin	2001	Design and Art direction: Tom Hingston Studio

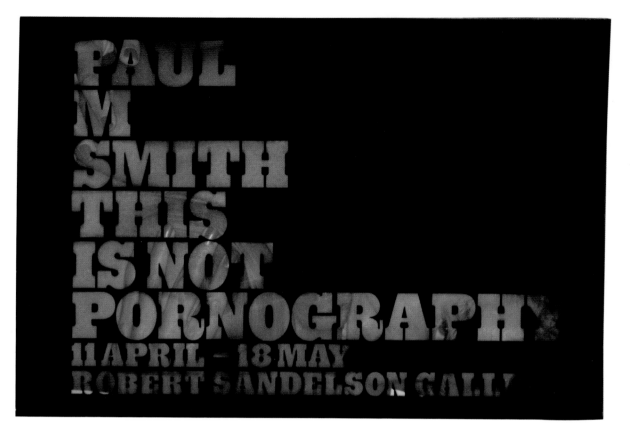

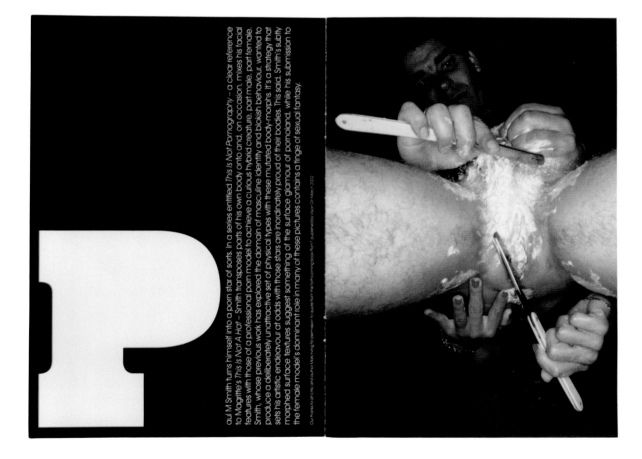

aul M Smith turns himself into a porn star of sorts. In a series entitled *This Is Not Pornography* – a clear reference to Magritte's *This Is Not A Hat* – Smith transposes parts of his own body onto and, on occasion, mixes his facial features with those of a professional porn model to achieve a curious hybrid creature, part male, part female. Smith, whose previous work has explored the domain of masculine identity and blokish behaviour, wanted to produce a deliberately unattractive set of physical types with these mutated body-morphs. It's a strategy that sets his artistic endeavour at odds with those stars are inordinately proud of their bodies. This said, Smith's subtly morphed surface textures suggest something of the surface glamour of pornoland, while his submission to the female model's dominant role in many of these pictures contains a tinge of sexual fantasy.

1		
2		

PAUL M SMITH EXHIBITION INVITE   Paul M Smith   2002   Design and Art direction: Tom Hingston Studio

PAUL M SMITH EXHIBITION INVITE / Spread   Paul M Smith   2002   Design and Art direction: Tom Hingston Studio

1			'TO BE CONFIRMED' SHOW INVITES / Various	To Be Confirmed	2002	Design and Art direction: Tom Hingston Studio
2			'TO BE CONFIRMED' SHOW INVITES / Various	To Be Confirmed	2001	Design and Art direction: Tom Hingston Studio
3			'TO BE CONFIRMED' SHOW INVITES / Various	To Be Confirmed	2002	Design and Art direction: Tom Hingston Studio

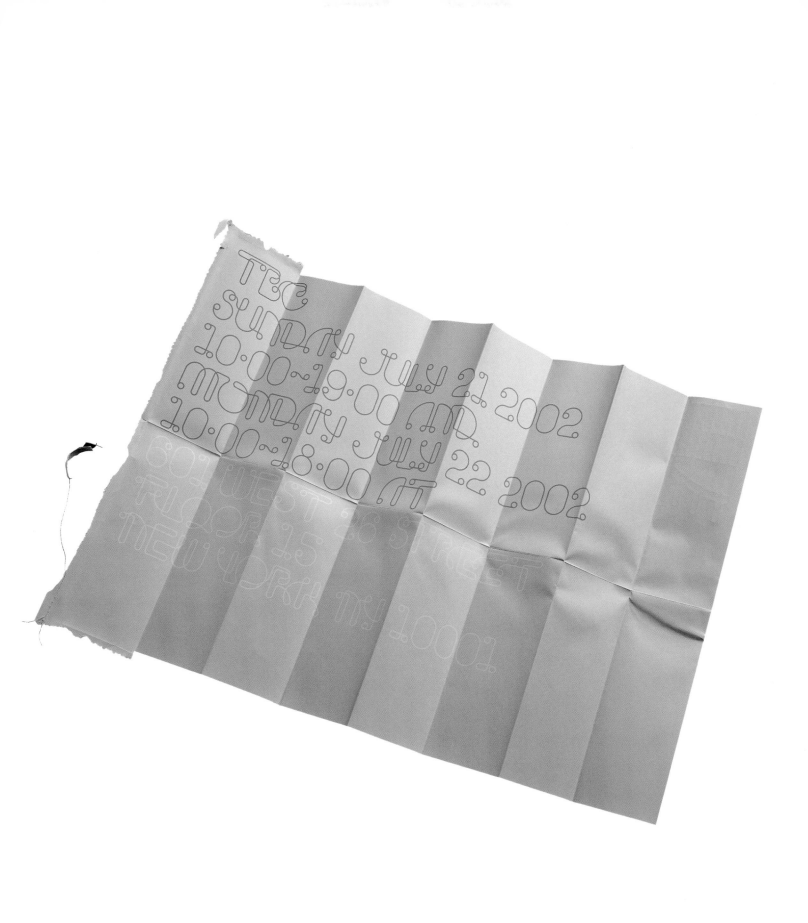

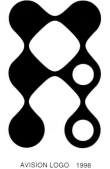

AVISION LOGO   1998
Avision

AFRO ART LOGO   1995
Afro Art

ANOKHA LOGO   1996
Blue Note Club

BLUE NOTE LOGO   1995
Blue Note Club

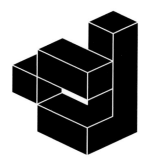

DETAIL FROM DEGEGNERATE T-SHIRT   2000

'DEGENERATE' LOGO   1999
Degenerate

DETAIL FROM DEGEGNERATE T-SHIRT   2001

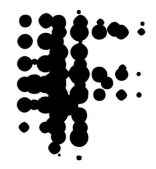

'FILTER RECORDS' LOGO   1995
Dorado Records

'IFONE' LOGO   2001
Avision

'KATHERINE HAMNETT' LOGO   1995
Katherine Hamnett

'NUPHONIC' LOGO   1995
Nuphonic

'ON THE DOG' LOGO   2000
On the Dog

LOGOS / Various

Design and Art direction: Tom Hingston Studio

OST LOGO 1998
Original Soundtrack Recordings

PLANET FUNK LOGO 2000
Virgin

POINT BLANK LOGO 1998
Point Blank

SATORI LOGO 1998
R&S Records

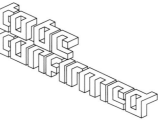

'SPACEK' LOGO 2001
Universal / Island

TBC LOGO 2001
To Be Confirmed

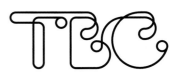

TBC LOGO 2002
To Be Confirmed

TBC LOGO 2002
To Be Confirmed

'WEST' LOGO 1999
West Management

'WISHAKISMO' LOGO 2001
EMI

'ZOOT WOMAN' LOGO 2000
Wall of Sound

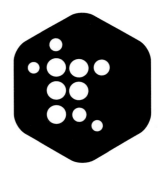

OWN LOGO 1996

[TOM
HINGSTON
STUDIO]

OWN LOGO 1998

13 02 16 MON 00:43 FAX 🖉001

Tom Hingston Studio Ltd

ANSWERS

[TOM
HINGSTON
STUDIO]

TO _AYAKO TERASHIMA — GASBOOK_

SUBJECT _ANSWERS.._

DATE _7/1/03_ PAGES INCLUDING THIS ONE ①

01 When do you most feel the presence of "design" around you??

• • • •

02 What is your favourite shape?

◯

03 What was your happiest moment in your work experience?

Five past six.

04 Please list up your 3 favourite colours?

Orange / Grey / Brown

~~05 What do you hate the most?~~

06 Please list up your 3 favourite materials.

Wood / Concrete / Wool

07 Where is your most favourite place?

Home

08 Please list up your 3 favourite designers?

Wim Crouwel / Ralph Lauren / Charles &
Ray Eames.

09 Please define the word "design".

Thought

10 Please list up your 3 favourite words.

Love / Surface / Rhythm

Registered Office

EDITORIAL CREDIT

GASBOOK 04
TOM HINGSTON STUDIO

COVER DESIGN TOM HINGSTON STUDIO
COVOR PHOTO Paul Wetherell

EDITORIAL DIRECTOR Toru Hachiga
CONTRIBUTING EDITOR & TEXT Daniel Mason
ART DIRECTOR Hideki Inaba
DESIGNER Takanobu Niizeki, Tadamune Yamagata
COORDINATOR Ayako Terashima

EXECUTIVE PRODUCER Takeyuki Fujii
PRODUCER Akira Natsume

PUBLISHER Masanori Omae

Image ©TOM HINGSTON STUDIO 2003
©2003 DesignEXchange Co.,Ltd.

Published in Japan in 2003 and distributed worldwide by DesignEXchange Co.,Ltd.
Nakameguro GS Dai2 Bldg 2-9-35 Kamimeguro Meguro-ku Tokyo 153-0051 Japan
Phone 81 3 5704 7350   Fax 81 3 5704 7351
e-mail pggas@dex.ne.jp
http://www.dex.ne.jp

ISBN 4-86083-264-7

Printed in Japan by Toppan Printing Co.,Ltd.

First Printing, 2003

PAGE 62 and 63

1			TOM HINGSTON STUDIO	PHOTO James Harris
2	2	1	QUESTION	